Girls Are
Coming Out
of the Woods

Girls Are Coming Out of the Woods

TISHANI DOSHI

COPPER CANYON PRESS
PORT TOWNSEND, WASHINGTON

Copper Canyon Press is in residence at Fort Worden State Park in Port Townsend, Washington, under the auspices of Centrum. Centrum is a gathering place for artists and creative thinkers from around the world, students of all ages and backgrounds, and audiences seeking extraordinary cultural enrichment.

First published in hardback in India in 2017 by HarperCollins *Publishers* India

LIBRARY OF CONGRESS CATALOGING-IN-PUBLICATION DATA
Names: Doshi, Tishani, 1975- author.
Title: Girls are coming out of the woods / Tishani Doshi.
Description: Port Townsend, Washington : Copper Canyon Press, [2018]
Identifiers: LCCN 2018005991| ISBN 9781556595516 (hardback : alk. paper) |
ISBN 9781556595509 (pbk. : alk. paper)
Classification: LCC PR9499.4.D67 A6 2018 | DDC 821/.92--dc23
LC record available at https://lccn.loc.gov/2018005991

Copper Canyon Press
Post Office Box 271
Port Townsend, Washington 98368
www.coppercanyonpress.org

for my mother, Eira,
born in snow,
bold as roses.

The fox drags its wounded belly
Over the snow, the crimson seeds
Of blood burst with a mild explosion,
Soft as excrement, bold as roses.

— R.S. Thomas, 'January'

CONTENTS

Girls Are
Coming Out
of the Woods

Contract

Dear Reader,
I agree to turn my skin inside out,
to reinvent every lost word, to burnish,
to steal, to do what I must
in order to singe your lungs.

I will forgo happiness,
stab myself repeatedly,
and lower my head into countless ovens.

I will fade backwards into the future
and tell you what I see.
If it is bleak, I will lie
so that you may live
seized with wonder.
If it is miraculous, I will
send messages in your dreams,
and they will flicker
as a silvered cottage in the woods,
choked with vines of moonflower.

Don't kill me, Reader.
This neck has been working for years
to harden itself against the axe.
This body, meagre as it is,
has lost so many limbs to wars, so many
eyes and hearts to romance. But love me,
and I will follow you everywhere—
to the dusty corners of childhood,
to every downfall and resurrection.
Till your skin becomes my skin.
Let us be twins, our blood
thumping after each other
like thunder and lightning.
And when you put your soft head
down to rest, dear Reader,
I promise to always be there,
humming in the dungeons
of your auditory canals—
an immortal mosquito,
hastening you towards fury,
towards incandescence.

Summer in Madras

Everyone in the house is dying.
Mother in an air-conditioned room
cannot hear as rivers break their dams
against her nerves. Father stalks verandas,
offering pieces of his skin to the rows of lurid
gulmohars. Husband tries to still the advancing
armies of the past by stuffing his ears with desiccated
mango husks. And brother? Brother is most lackadaisical of all.
He opens the door. Takes death's umbrella. Taps it this way and that. Sings.

Rain at Three

Rain at three splits the bed in half,
cracks at windows like horsemen blistering
through a century of hibernation.
The washing's on the line.
There are pillows in the grass.
All the weeds we pulled up yesterday
lie in clotted heaps, dying slowly.
We sleep with pumiced, wooden
bodies—mud-caked, mud-brown,
listening to the fan-whir sea-heave
of our muscled Tamil Nadu nights.
We turn inwards
announce how patiently
we've waited for this uprooting.
Now that damaged petals of hibiscus
drown the terrace stones,
we must kneel together and gather.
This is how desire works:
splintering first, then joining.

A Fable for the 21st Century

Existing is plagiarism. — E.M. Cioran

There is no end to unknowing.
We read papers. Wrap fish in yesterday's news,
spread squares on the floor so puppy can pee
on Putin's face. Even the mountains cannot say
what killed the Sumerians all those years ago.
And as such, you should know that blindness
is historical, that nothing in this poem will make
you thinner, richer, or smarter. Myself—
I couldn't say how a light bulb worked,
but if we threw you headfirst into the past,
what would you say about the secrets
of chlorophyll? How would you expound
on the aggression of sea anemones,
the Battle of Plassey, Boko Haram?
Language is a peculiar destiny.
                    Once, at the desert's edge,
a circle of pilgrims spoke of wonder—
their lives dark with mud and hoes.
They didn't know you could make perfume
from rain, that human blood was more fattening
than beer. But their fears were ripe and lucent,
their clods of children plentiful, and God
walked among them, knitting sweaters

for injured chevaliers. Will you tell them
how everything that's been said is worth
saying again? How the body is helicoidal,
spiriting on   and   on
How it is only ever through the will of nose,
bronchiole, trachea, lung,
that breath outpaces
any sadness
of tongue

What the Sea Brought In

Brooms, brassieres, empty bottles
of booze. The tip of my brother's
missing forefinger. Bulbs, toothpaste caps,
instruments for grooming. Chestnuts,
carcass of coconut, crows, crabs.
Three dying fish, four dead grandparents.
Slippers of every stripe: rubber, leather,
Rexine, felt. Rope, mollusc, baleen, foam.
Two ghost children foraging their way
home. The Bootchie Man, budgerigars,
a pack of poor poisoned dogs. Keys,
spoons, singular socks. Virginity returned
in a chastity box. Letters of love,
letters of lust, the 1980s, funeral dust.
What the sea brought in was enough
to fill museums—decapitated marigold,
broken nautilus, a betrayed school friend
stuck in the dunes like the legs of Ozymandias.
Park benches, milk teeth, snake-skins,
cartwheels. Somewhere in the many years
of waking given over to sleep: a cavalcade
of cognitions, a mustard jumpsuit.
If everything we've lost were to return
with the sea, how simply we could offer
our sun-scarred lives, our soiled mattresses.

Such solace to know that barnacles house
empires, that the feral creature of love
grows from gravestones of breakers,
blooms like wildflowers in the fetch.

How to be Happy in 101 Days

Adore stone. Learn to manoeuvre
against the heat of things. Should
you see butterflies gambol in the air,
resist the urge to pinch their wings.
Look for utilitarian values of violence.
Use the knife lustily: to peel the mango's
jealous skin, to wean bark and cut bread
for the unending hunger of stray dogs.
Renounce your house. Take just one
object with you. Slip it in your pocket.
Marvel at how a simple thing can
connect the variegated skeins of time.
On the 99th day, you must surrender
this object, but until then feel free
to attach sentiment to it. Find a forest
to disappear in. Look for thirst-quenching
plants. Rub the smooth globes of their roots
in your palms before biting into their hearts.
Lean backwards and listen to the slippery
bastard of your own arrhythmic heart.
Remind yourself that you feel pain,
therefore you must be alive. Stain
your fingers with ink. Set out into
the world and prepare to be horrified.
Do not close your eyes. Catch a fish.

Smash its head and watch the life gasp
out of it. Spit the bones into sand.
Offer your bones to someone.
Clavicles are the chief seducers
of the human body. When you hear
the snap, allow yourself a shudder.
Find a tree to hold all the faces
of your dead—their hair, their rings.
Hang their solemn portraits from branches.
If you cannot find happiness in death
you will not complete the course.
Give your child to a stranger.
If you are childless, offer the person
you love best. Do not ask about possible
ways of mistreatment. Trust it will be terrible.
Climb a mountain. Feel how much larger
the world is when you're alone.
Try to find words or images
to explain your loss. Give up. Stand on your head.
Grow dizzy on your own blood.
Spend the night in a cemetery.
Keep still and listen to the dead chortle.
Tattoo your face. Do not bother with stars.
They are for romantics (who are not happy
people). Learn to steer through darkness.
If you're attacked, spread your legs and say,
Brother, why are you doing this to me?
When you approach a crossing in the woods,

take the one instinct tells you to take.
When you are knee-deep in mud, turn
around and try the other path in order
to understand how little you know
of yourself. In a few days you'll be ready
for the sublime. Before that, meditate
in a cave. If a tigress finds you, offer her
the meat of your thighs, give her cubs
your breasts. If tigers are already extinct,
wait for some other hairy, hungry creature
to accost you. It will happen.
It is important for you to lose both
body and mind. Dig a hole in the earth
with your hands. Place your treasured
object in it and thrill at how little
it means to let it go. On the 101st
day, search out a mirror. Strip
away your clothes. Inch up to
your reflection. Much of the success
of this course will depend on what you see.

Fear Management

Say it is dawn on the beach
and you are without the dogs.
Up ahead, a row of fishermen.
Legs like pins, tomb-sized chests,
leaning back on their heels to haul.
Say they are making noises at you.
A sideways kind of sound designed
to entice a small, brainless creature
into a corner before smashing it
underfoot. And above their noise,
the rattle of boats thudding across water,
bee-eaters, the despair of an early
morning dream, where you relinquished
your life as if it were of no consequence.

All you can see is the sun, orange and whole,
rising like a guillotine into the sky. Beneath,
an ocean's regurgitations—

                          orphaned slippers,
             styrofoam, fossil of crab,
and the fishermen dragging their nets
against the lip of all this
with their ceaseless, cooing threats.

When so much can be vanished
so silently into the dark teeth of sleep,
tell me, wouldn't you fear for your life?
What it is. What it might become.

Everyone Loves a Dead Girl

They arrive at parties alone because they are dead
now and there is nothing to fear except for the sun,
except for the rustle of tablecloths, which instigates
a quickening in them, the reminder of a tip-tap
phantom heart. They are beautiful, so when they stand
beside lampshades or murals, rooms shrink, and the air,
previously content to swan around in muddy shorts,
grows disgruntled and heavy. They discuss methods
of dying because even though there can be no repetition
of that experience, something about the myth of the peaceful
bed annoys them. They would like to tell people how naïve
death wishes are. They feel an exhibition of *Wounds You Never*
Thought Imaginable might help contextualize things. A girl—
call her my own, call her my lovely, stands up and says,
I would like to talk about what it means to suffocate on pillow
feathers, to have your neck held like a cup of wine, all delicate
and beloved, before it is crushed. Another stands, and another,
and even though they have no names and some of them
have satin strips instead of faces, they all have stories
which go on and on—ocean-like, glamorous, until
it is morning and they go wherever it is dead girls go.

In the parties of the real world, people talk about how some
girls walk down the wrong roads and fall down rabbit holes.
People who haven't put their faces in the soft stomach
of another's for years, who no longer go out at night
to chase the moon. Even those people who do nothing
but make love in grass all day long. Benevolent people.
Their hearts leap when they hear a story of a dead girl,
and when they tell it to someone (how could they not?)
the telling is a kind of nourishing—all the dormant bits
inside them charge around like Bolshoi dancers re-entering
the world alive, and with wonder. Because how could you not
hold on to your wrists and listen to *that that that*
unquestionable bloom? How could you not fall apart
with relief? And when they hold their own girls close,
maybe they tell them how beauty is a distance
they don't need to travel. Maybe they make braids
of their daughters' hair, and while doing this, imagine
they could be secured. Truly, they believe themselves when they say,
the world is a forest, darling, remember the bread crumbs,
remember to dig a tunnel home through the rain.

Monsoon Poem

Because this is a monsoon poem
expect to find the words jasmine,
palmyra, *Kuruntokai*, red; mangoes
in reference to trees or breasts; paddy
fields, peacocks, Kurinji flowers,
flutes; lotus buds guarding love's
furtive routes. Expect to hear a lot
about erotic consummation inferred
by laburnum gyrations and bamboo
syncopations. Listen to the racket
of wide-mouthed frogs and bent-
legged prawns going about their
business of mating while rain falls
and falls on tiled roofs and verandas,
courtyards, pagodas. Because such
a big part of you seeks to understand
this kind of rain—so unlike your cold
rain, austere rain, get-me-the-hell-
out-of-here rain. Rain that can't fathom
how to liberate camphor from the vaults
of the earth. Let me tell you how little
is written of mud, how it sneaks up
like a sleek-gilled vandal to catch hold
of your ankles. Or about the restorative
properties of mosquito blood, dappled

and fried against the wires of a bug-zapping
paddle. So much of monsoon is to do
with being overcome—not from longing
as you might think, but from the sky's
steady bludgeoning, until every leaf
on every unremembered tree gleams
in the abyss of post-coital bliss.
Come. Now sip on your masala tea,
put your lips to the sweet, spicy skin
of it. There's more to see—notice
the dogs who've been fucking on the beach,
locked in embrace like an elongated Anubis,
the crabs scavenging the flesh of a dopey-
eyed ponyfish, the entire delirious coast
with its philtra of beach and saturnine
clouds arched backwards in disbelief.
And the mayflies who swarm in November
with all their ephemeral grandeur to die
in millions at the behest of light, the geckos
stationed on living room walls, cramming
fistfuls of wings in their maws. Notice
how hardly anyone mentions the word
death, even though the fridge leaks
and the sheets have been damp for weeks.
And in this helter-skelter multitude
of grey-greenness, notice how even the rain
begins to feel fatigued. The roads and sewers
have nowhere to go, and like old-fashioned pursuers

they wander and spill their babbling hearts
to electrical poles and creatures with ears.
And what happens later, you might ask,
after we've moved to a place of shelter,
when the cracks in the earth have reappeared?
We dream of wet, of course, of being submerged
in millet stalks, of webbed toes and stalled
clocks and eels in the mouth of a heron.
We forget how unforgivably those old poems
led us to believe that men were mountains,
that the beautiful could never remain
heartbroken, that when the rains arrive
we should be delighted to be taken
in drowning, in devotion.

Ode to Patrick Swayze

At fourteen I wanted to devour you,
the twang, the strut, the perfect proletarian
butt in the black pants of you. I wanted a man
like you to sashay into town and teach me
how to be an aeroplane in water. I didn't want
to be a baby. I wanted to be your baby.
I wanted revenge. I wanted to sue my breasts
for not living up to potential. I wanted Jennifer Grey
to meet with an unfortunate end and not have a love affair
with a ghost. At fourteen, I believed you'd given birth
to the word preternatural, and when Mother came
home one day, waving her walking shoe, saying,
I lost my soul in the Theosophical Society,
I wanted to dance as recklessly as the underside
of that shoe. I wanted to be a pebble in the soft
heel of you. To horse-whisper and live on a ranch
in Texas and love my blonde wife forever and have
creases around my eyes and experience at least one
goddamn summer where I could be like the wind—
sexy and untrammelled and dirty. And it was only
after I found my own Johnny (and got rid of him),
only yesterday, when I rescued a northern shoveler
from crows on the beach, his broken wing
squished against the crockery of my ribs,
only after setting him down at the edge

of a canal, where he sank in to the long patient
task of dying, that I realized what I'd wanted
most was to be held by someone determined
to save me, someone against whom I could press
my unflourishing chest, who'd offer me
not just the time of my life, but who'd tear
out reams of his yellowing pancreas,
and say, *Here, baby, eat.*

Abandon

There must be a word for a person
who longs to run into the eye
of a storm, a word for every tree
that lies slaughtered on the streets
after a cyclone. A word like lachrymose
or pulmonary. A word for they have left
you alone to face your doom. In Aleppo.
In Aleppo. I cannot speak of Aleppo.
Only that it is the opposite of breath.
There must be a word for the walk
home at night. Your belongings in two bags,
feet in mud. For a family thinking they will return.
Maybe the house still stands. Maybe the sea.
The dead leave no clues about what lies beyond.
We call it eternal. We call it now.

To My First White Hairs

*Weave then, weave o quickly weave
your sham veneration. Knit me webs of winter sagehood,
nightcap, and the fungoid sequins of a crown.* — Wole Soyinka

Dear Sirs,
I wish you'd arrived sooner.
I've been waiting since 1983.
HQ sent a notice of disapproval.
A seven-year-old, they wrote, has scant
need to speak of emulating Indira
Gandhi's signature white streak.
But still, it would have been nice
to have heard from you directly.
Being a woman has its challenges
as you know, and if you're power
hungry, all the more so. In this
country the Madonna–whore
conundrum is just a glum
preamble to the vast savageries
of patriarchy. The sole way
to achieve female domination
is to sacrifice motherhood
with finality along with any
stray blooms of sexuality.
To keep tiny sprigs of glamour

at bay by assuming a matronly
shape and martyr's position.
Each year I waited for signs
of decline. I worried and raged
so intensely the weight slid
off me like a dictionary,
(which in these anorexic times
worked against me—adding
cheekbone definition instead
of desired Titian dimensions).
In my thirties, crow's feet turned up
in fabulous attendance but not
enough to deter the proboscises
of wannabe husbands. Dear Sirs,
I longed for your arrival in every
muddy confluence of life, watched
the conveyor belt of decrepitude
make rickety journeys around
ladies less worthy. I waited,
and in the waiting subjected
myself to multiple shocks
and incidents of strife,
hoping to suddenly go white.
I grew out my hair and butchered it,
straightened and permed it,
laid out in the sun and fried it,
(although I admit, I regularly

oiled it). I even experimented
with alternative trademarks—
saffron saris and bullet-proof
capes but neither approach
hit quite the right mark.

And suddenly, you're here.
So cavalier! To arrive in the most
self-loving city in the world.
Two white hairs leaping
like samurais from the frontiers
of forty, your silver swords
gleaming from bandoliers,
reflected as swirls in the grand
canal of this most serene
of republics. The irony
isn't lost on me. Dear Sirs,
you know I'd sing paeans
if I could, but let's not be twee
about the state of affairs.
Upon your arrival it's become
quite clear that the circle
of life is in fact a square,
that the particularity of yearning
is such that desires are inverted
as soon as they appear.
So forgive me for not singing

myself hoarse in the fashion
of a maudlin gondolier.
I'd thank you, white hairs,
as a poet should,
but I'm too busy catching
my breath on the stairs.

Considering Motherhood While Falling
Off a Ladder in Rome

In the Via della Scala in Rome,
in one of those apartments
tourists dream of owning,
I walked down a ladder
in my underwear,
with a bottle in one hand
and an apple in the other.
And when I fell,
it was with turbulence,
with knowledge,
that every rib of shame
would smash against the floor,
that ambivalence was primeval.

Later, when we walked
across the Tiber to bring
your son home from school,
we paused to watch birds
in the sky—starlings
in the thousands.
And I could not explain
that it was the beating
of their wings,
the murmurations,

that were a kind of drowning.
That I too would chew
at the bark
of life, if it would
bequeath me fire.

It was November,
the season of death,
and the river moved darkly
between her banks,
the birds flew from sycamore
to sycamore like tapestry,
flood. And every epiphany
that has since arrived
has yielded only in breath,
tempestuous, forbidden breath.

Love in the Time of Autolysis

When you die, Love, I will leave you out
like a Zoroastrian, listen to the hiss
of oxygen withdraw, watch your blood
pool and glister while protein filaments
lock, and stiffness strikes your eyelids,
neck, jaw. And I will touch—of course,
I will touch your discoloured skin,
your beard, the sundry coils of hair,
as your body morphs from man to farm.
It will almost kill me to see the swarms
of blowflies colonize the fens and flower-
beds of your nose, mushrooms vaulting
from the mud of abdomen, skin so blue
and mottled, the bloat and putrefaction.
But darling, what of ruined flesh?
Of scorpion flies making Bloody Marys
and Bellinis from the dregs of brain fluid?
These bacterial passengers, ancient druids,
have left migration tracks along the furrows
of your gut, built kingdoms in the outposts
of your capillaries, spilled so much blood.
Those in the know call it *thanatomicrobiome*,
but we know it as something else, this ecosystem
feeding on the country of you as sheets of skin
slip like glaciers, and the purge begins.

There is nothing secret or impure about
your death, but still, I come in darkness
to lay my words like eggs in the wounds
of your orifices. And what my words mean
to say is that I am bereft, that I long
for the myth of sunlight in a room—
my head against your chest, the ghost
of your beating heart. The sky will be
here soon to adorn herself with you.
She is jealous of our history, of our
afternoons of whispered Ungaretti.
When she comes, Love, I will lie with you.
We will be dead stars again, thumbs entwined,
looking back at the mystery of ourselves.

Jungian Postcard

Dear Carl, the days here are impossible:
all silence, and the sea. Yesterday we saw
the horizon unstitch itself from the sky
so delicately, and further down the beach,
two stray dogs materialized like lost souls
from a genie's lamp. I just had to cry.

Our anima and animus! My love cried,
being philosophically inclined and impossible
to argue with. But the way those bony animal souls
took ownership of us—one black, one gold, and saw
fit to flex their paws on that deserted beach,
unmoved by the disentangled sky

that had banished all its birds. The sky
that slumped so languidly into the sea. I had to cry
for all my complexes. I won't deny, this beach
brought out strange things in me: impossibilities.
And the silence! Such eviscerating silence. We saw
no boats in sight, or bees. Just us, our souls

and the sea. Funny, those flea-bag souls
of ours, appearing out of nowhere like the sky
just deciding enough's enough. Carl, I saw
what I saw. And the whole thing made me cry
because no matter how magical, it was impossible—
the restlessness reared up. I had to leave the beach.

Stay, my love said. *Let's make castles on the beach.*
But I could only think of our hungry souls
and what to feed them. How impossibly
they wandered from beach to beach, the sky
their only sanctuary. It made me cry
for my love and me, our unrelenting see-saw

about where to live and who to be. I saw
no glimpse of destiny on that nameless beach
with our anima and animus except to cry
because we *would* have homeless souls
wouldn't we? And underneath that gleaming sky,
how skinny they looked, how impossible.

Carl, I left the beach to go inside to cry and from
the gate, I saw my love devotedly restore the hem of sky;
two souls resting at his feet, perfect in their possibilities.

Girls Are Coming Out of the Woods

for Monika

Girls are coming out of the woods,
wrapped in cloaks and hoods,
carrying iron bars and candles
and a multitude of scars, collected
on acres of premature grass and city
buses, in temples and bars. Girls
are coming out of the woods
with panties tied around their lips,
making such a noise, it's impossible
to hear. Is the world speaking too?
Is it really asking, *What does it mean
to give someone a proper resting?* Girls are
coming out of the woods, lifting
their broken legs high, leaking secrets
from unfastened thighs, all the lies
whispered by strangers and swimming
coaches, and uncles, especially uncles,
who said spreading would be light
and easy, who put bullets in their chests
and fed their pretty faces to fire,
who sucked the mud clean
        off their ribs, and decorated
their coffins with briar. Girls are coming
out of the woods, clearing the ground

to scatter their stories. Even those girls
found naked in ditches and wells,
those forgotten in neglected attics,
and buried in river beds like sediments
from a different century. They've crawled
their way out from behind curtains
of childhood, the silver-pink weight
of their bodies pushing against water,
against the sad, feathered tarnish
of remembrance. Girls are coming out
of the woods the way birds arrive
at morning windows—pecking
and humming, until all you can hear
is the smash of their miniscule hearts
against glass, the bright desperation
of sound—bashing, disappearing.
Girls are coming out of the woods.
They're coming. They're coming.

Strong Men, Riding Horses

after Gwendolyn Brooks

The men in my life come back strong.
Fat off the agony of summers gone, these men
no longer think to write or call before riding
into dreams with Lugers and Stetsons. On horses.
All wrong. They charge in. They charge in
like assassins through floorboards and fairings. The
men in my life grow spring-like out West.
Cowboys with taches and gingham chests, adrift on
the lawns of banishment. O, the infinity of a
grown man who waits. The candidates range
from primate to giant. Faces morose as funerals. Five
years unravel into five hundred.
So many disappeared miles.
The men in my life hold secrets like spears. A
thousand
would-be husbands circle the border, reaching
for navel, face, breastplate, rope. And from
everything you imagined that was not, comes dawn,
spidery and wet, releasing them back to
the West, to where they rode in from. Sunset
restores them with harmonicas, rested
and keen for a-battering again. Yesterday's blue-
tongued blades of grass. All the paths to
longing are recurring and paved with orange

trees, earthquakes, other women's men. From
here the future blooms like a prehistoric fish of hope:
flat-headed, obdurate. The lesson being to
submerge, to listen to the music of bones crying
as they are changed from gills to hoof. Except
for the fossils gathered at our feet, that
insist with an architecture ancient and strong,
what can we say about empires of harmony, of men
who ride horses? Treacherous as they are,
we must counter these phantoms, desert-eyed.
Except
for sleep, nothing is ever finished, and all that
remains of night is a rooftop in summer, a strong
wind from the sea, birds, hay, a family of men
with high foreheads, picking their teeth. They are
lurching toward you with balsam and pasted-
down hair. Breath jangly with fear. To
have survived the ever-present restlessness of stars.
Wake now. All that we mourn is here already.

Disco Biscuits

We were talking about the subject of Quaaludes,
of which I know nothing except back in the 70s,
when I was being born, Bill Cosby slipped them
to a bunch of women. When I think of the past
like that I think of a child hiding under the staircase
among the family's dusty shoes, a pair of discontented
lampshades. How most of us have known a man
who arrived like Bill—sleek and proud as a July
thunderstorm. How so many of us gave in to that sleekness
because when you're young you don't know that your bones
have been giving way the second you were born. So you give,
and your giving's large and uncalculated. But then
there's the haunting. And how it works is a kind of time warp
that bitch-slaps you when you're at your innocent best,
like this morning in the dance theatre, which is all mongoose-
hurry, ant-scurry and slow slowing down. I was going for that
out-of-body experience with navel to floor, toes to ceiling. I
heard the sap rise in the frills of those indefatigable shrubs,
the crows going on with their cawing, the sea in the distance,
beautiful in her reiterations. I heard time cracking at his knees,
and suddenly, kablam, I'm seventeen, and everyone has
something to hide. The church at the corner folding in on itself,
a vagrant fiddling with the pleats of his loincloth. Even
the lampposts are desperate to tuck in their ungainly feet.
The city and her persiflage. The acres of burning sand.

Listen now, as the wind caterwauls like a deranged megaphone.
All our old selves are parading the beach, whispering how
there should be a museum for this kind of installation.
They're crushing bits of nostalgia in their heels. They grow
photophobic and bendy. They splinter. They shirr.

Honesty Hotel for Gents

I imagine them arriving for dinner in this dolorous city
of mine, emerging from AC & non-AC rooms in pant-shirts
and patchouli perfume. Are they here for a convention
on niceness, these mustachioed gents, who long
for the leathery glory of bread, but instead, must confess
their shortcomings over rasam and rice? Is their loneliness
a strip of whalebone stuck in the collar of a shirt no one will
wear? Or are their lovers multifarious, lying askew on beds,
pleading, *Just this once, tell us a lie!* And can they really
explain how shame is a building with a hundred and one
doors, how to be in the club you have to open and open?
Do they venerate their mothers? They must. These men
who button and unbutton. Is there a secret handshake
to identify others of the tribe—a discernible nobility
of fingernails? O woodcutters, there are no gods to retrieve
your axes from the rivers of this town. A man is born,
and then what? He finds himself on the streets of Madras.
Somewhere a van is rounding up dogs and cane-ribbed cats.
Somewhere a temple with multiple chins is sheltering
a fishing bird and a million prevarications. Do they believe
in the integrity of shadows? Their own being earnest
and loyal, but skulking after all, in the fashion of shadows.
Because I'm still thinking the world is thuggish as dirt,
how none of this decreases our collective dread. Weep,
honest men! We are all responsible for graveyards of old

toothbrushes and the stowage of wayward languages.
We stamp and dance, drift from here to there, but a city
will come when we must rest in our contradictions,
spread the motor oil of gloom on our bones, give in
to waterlogged roads and cortèges of flowers.

My Grandmother Never Ate a Potato in Her Life

I can't be sure, but I like the shock
of it, the irrationality
of not wanting to harm the unseen
bacteria underground.
The abstinence of tuber.
My grandmother (even though
I was told never to begin
a poem with grandmother)
wore big glasses and enjoyed
diamonds and cards. She made
deer of her fingers, and peacocks.
As a girl she wore ribbons
in her plaits. I miss her even though
it has been so long since I knew her.
I think of her great care towards ants,
of the shiny coins she slipped me.
Of the words I take from her mouth
and paste into imaginary notebooks.
The TV blares and my brother reclines
like a baby god, watching cartoons,
straining his fragile neck.
We are in the house alone together
and it is everything I've ever feared.
The soft night of Madras pushing
her sweaty chest towards us,
saying, see how alone,
you and him and her.

Your Body Language Is Not Indian! *or* Where I Am Snubbed at a Cocktail Party by a Bharatnatyam Dancer

Lady, do you know how long I've roamed
this world like a saw-toothed shrew, sans hubby
and kids? Do you understand the kind of resistance
involved in arriving at 37—alone, two white hairs,
the onset of wrinkles. To have withstood barricades
of scolding aunties and so many diabolical winters
of social conditioning? To have said N-O
to the effervescent sortie of evolution,
which twitches in me even as I cling to a puppy,
or sing lullabies to birds. I've thought about it,
sure—of a warm body that might save me,
of these teeth of mine, which could go on and on.
But I bowed out of the race, said thanks, but no,
to History and Biology. I decline the invitation
to breed. And when the situation got aggressive,
I gave a giant finger to Genes, to centuries
of women before me who patiently flexed
their shoulders and hoiked up their knees.
To all of them I've written letters of apology.
And before all this, Lady, I was a teenager!
No picnic, as you know—a decade of crawling
through slums in the gloaming; all those neuroses
and goddamn deficiencies. How many nights

of fevered fantasies? And before that—
childhood—transparent days
of burrow and play. Being carted around
like a lady's lapdog, peeing and being petted,
paying no heed to the hours in the woods,
to subterranean skills of survival and moulting.
And this is saying nothing of the tremendous
caravan of Time, which mutters velvet aphorisms
as you sleep, like, *In extreme solitude men perceive
again the touch of immortal wings*. Or, *Civilization seems
to be the invention of a species now extinct*.
So, having arrived this far, spare me, please,
if I choose to be mysterious. If I delight
in dilutions and the vagaries of neither here
nor there, and display no seals of authenticity.
What right have I, after all? Part sea creature,
part peach tree, to take this cocktail chatter
seriously? But Lady, truly, you offend,
when you say: *Your body language is not Indian!*
You demolish me by quartering my paltry
ancestry into territories of wetland, desert,
marsh, city. My legs and arms, banished,
poor things, for incorrect mudras and aramandis.
And why? Because I refuse to wear the sins
of my progenitors in the topography of my chin?
Because the wobble of my head is too perfunctory?
Must I be more like you, who has so clearly
embezzled the coronary stance of your turgid

mama and faint-hearted papa; who carries
all those failed proteins in your body
like an identity card? And just how far
will you go to ensure generations of Bharatnatyam
domination? Eliminate me if you must,
for I will always prefer the pale underside
of the past to a future of grass. And when
I die, which is a fate no mammal can escape,
it will be far from home in a nest underground.
There will be tremors and some confusion
as I hang these muddy bracelets of existence
around the wrists of an easterly wind. We will dance,
the wind and I—our bodies like rosebushes alight
in the sky, clanging against the geometry of stars.

Saturday on the Scores

You begin alone, soft-footed.
Hair, an unruly halo of hedgerows.
The wind stings your chest,
unleashes a street of neat,
gleaming houses. In the distance,
an ice-cream stand, and the sea—
a beleaguered scrim of blue.
The body is just a cage,
but open one door, and the city
will offer her bones, shed colour.
Pull up the collar of your coat.
Tighten your belt. Know,
if you wanted, you could seduce
a stranger. Perhaps you have
already. He is walking beside you,
cigarette in hand, listening
to you talk of the tenderness
you feel towards the human ear;
how difficult it was, therefore,
for you to witness your mother's
ears growing—not monstrously,
but enough to mar her indivisible
beauty. He admits to loving
his father more, to wanting children,
not necessarily with his wife.

You agree on nothing except
to walk till you have collected
enough lost objects to fill
the minutes of Mozart's *Requiem.*
In the graveyard, one of you talks
of fire, how the soul must be endless.
The other wants a needle to thread roots
through the ligaments of the earth.
Each is an aberration. Must it rain?
Yes! Now, as the sky slips off
the girders, revealing a secret garden.
Light the rain falls. Light the dead.

The Women of the Shin Yang Park Sauna, Gwangju

Hello, I'm naked, the bubble above my head
says, translated into Korean for their benefit.
But they are busy with their breasts and cunts,
their dimpled, rounded, flat-dented buttocks,
busy washing disappointment from their houses
of sternum, busy with the dirt of summer lodged
around hillocks of elbow and whirlpools of navel.
In one room, a woman is pummelling another,
rubbing oil into her flanks and well-worn back.
In another, the young ones sit in a circle on stools.
Their breasts are Jell-O to gravity, they undulate
and lift, undulate and lift. There is gossiping,
of course, world over there is a posture
that involves gleam, that involves lean all the way
in for a proper bitching. *Hello, I'm naked
and I've washed.* The older women's bodies
are segregated by hysterectomy scars.
They murmur in hot tubs with headwraps,
legs spread like avenues of thick black trees.
They are warriors—plundered or having plundered.
The threat of annihilation sits in cool dishes
of water beside them. *Do you feel destroyed,
girl?* One of them looks at me the way death
might look at life, with pity and all the sweetness
reserved for a person who cannot be shown

the way out. She lifts a dish of water
and pours it over her head, barely flinches
from the iciness. *So this is how storms blow
through us.* She beckons with one finger.
Come, she seems to be saying. You are me,
I am you, neither one of us immaculate.

Tranås

So *this* is Sunday in Sweden.
We walk the drag like queens,
past furniture shops neatly sealed,
looking for sanatoriums, remnants
of Viking courts, trolls. Something
to reassure us we're not home.
A man drives by in a red Cadillac.
I want to hitch a ride to another life.
Down at the bottom of the lake
float the bodies of soldiers devastated
by plague, potato-rioters, a childhood
frock of Greta Garbo, the syphilitic ghost
of Eric Hermelin, whispering Hafez
to the fish. Come, visiting poets!
Listen as the day chafes across train
tracks, forging its own alphabet
of runes. And when sleep finally
descends on the fur factory,
skulking behind curtains of skin,
know that every bright night brings
with it, its own sideways thrum
of burdens and enchantments.

Encounters with a Swedish Burglar

The first night was a lark, something to break
the unbearable brightness of 3 a.m.
You kicked open the door with muddy boots,
stole chocolate, buns, a bottle of balsamico.
I think I scared you more—an apparition
in a white nightgown, bolted upright in bed
like that kid from *The Exorcist*. You shouted
something in Swedish and ran.

The second night you came back with friends,
smashed in the glass, cleared away hard drives
computers, keys. I heard you pace along the boards
of the dance studio like a troupe of myopic lions,
knocking over speakers, tripping on yoga mats.
You stayed clear of my bedroom, but left
a message on the stairs: a plate of chicken
with béarnaise sauce. EAT ME, it said.

The third night we activated the alarm.
I waited for the soft click of the door,
a lover's footsteps. And when they took
you away, I did not rush to see what kind
of boy you were. I walked around the house
instead, pocketing your first golden kiss,
a summer of jumping off rocks, tattoos, beards,
your father's Buick. And then I changed the locks.

Pig-Killing in Viet Hai

I remember the nipples,
a double row of pearls,
leading to the diamond
at her throat. Who needs
seven pairs of breasts?
These days I can't help
feel sick because they're still
pulling bodies out of rubble
in Nepal and the Duchess
has given birth to a girl.
The days follow each
other in secret the way
history slumps in fissures.
And so we watch movies,
hoping to reinstate our
lumpen hearts. Peter Sellers
in *The Party*—less funny
than when we saw it first.
Or Tarkovsky, brooding
and sepia-toned,
who tells us what we know:
that between the countries
of the mad and the sane
there's a ditch of water,
thin and sulphuric as piss.

My husband likes the word
dotard, and in this place
where we are both slowly
dying, there are monkeys
on balconies—their pink
bottoms, sore and enlarged.
Our dreams are filled with pig—
how a man slit her body from that
diamond wound, and everything
spilled—our innards, her innards,
the entrails, spleen and heart.
And even though it was done
tenderly, with a young boy
hauling buckets from the well
to clean the inconsistencies
of blood, even though the cliffs
stood green, the paddy gleamed,
and a woman walked her buffalo
home seemingly unconcerned—
She did not look dead, you see,
the hooves lurched forward
in a dance, even though
he was slicing away the skin,
deflating her—this coat
connected to the ribs like armour,
still, we would not call it slaughter.

And you can ask how it is possible
to live for days under rubble,
how babies caked with chalk and dust
emerge silently from houses.
We continue, despite
the aftershocks of loss,
to buy swimsuits online
for summer holidays.
You and I stay inside and read
Tolstoy, knowing it's a kind
of burial. The dog downstairs
barks, the fat kid in tracks
remains fat no matter how
many steps he climbs.
You can ask how they
could decapitate poor Orpheus,
poor pig from Viet Hai,
but it's only when he takes
the knife to the rough meat
of her neck and saws away
the head that she is altered
into something else. Bones,
back, rump, tail, going home
to sit on kitchen counters
in soggy paper bags.

Calcutta Canzone

For nights after I return from Calcutta,
there are piss-filled, shit-strewn dreams.
My brother, who has never been to Calcutta,
who knows nothing of the black holes of Calcutta,
lies in the room next door, while trees
sprout from rooftops in Calcutta
and a river of hock flows. In Calcutta
you'll find a poet on every corner, Brother!
At least, that's what they say. But my brother
sitting in the dark, isn't thinking of Calcutta,
or of poetry, or glorious decay.
He understands nothing of decay.

In Calcutta I bathe in tubs of decay.
Every dust-encrusted memory of Calcutta
is a lyric master class in decay.
As a poet I worship at the feet of decay,
fling myself at mottled skin. And in dreams,
I capitulate to orgies of Calcuttan decay
in mouldy palaces and boat houses. Even the decay
of a pelican going mad in his cage, or river trees
gnawing their way through sewers—all this is poetry
to me! But he is untouched by decay—
flipping his socks this way and that. My brother
with his punctured heart. My brother

who tunnels through the night. Brother,
why do you slam the doors? Tonight's decay
is as ruthless as a Bengali who hates Brother
Tagore. Sleep, my littlest of brothers.
I saw a boy like you in a street in Calcutta—
sleek-eyed, sweet, stocky, sanguine—brother
to someone, son. He was your shadow, brother,
like all the boys I've seen in my dreams.
It has to do with saving, or being saved. A dream
of redemption. And you are in them all, brother—
bougainvillea splaying from ruins. A tree
that grows in the shade of other trees.

And what has any of this to do with poetry?
I stalked the streets of Calcutta with a brother-
hood of poets, through graveyards with rocketing trees,
and for every dead and dying thing, we found a tree
that feathered lustily above the rust of trellises. *Decay
is a maudlin love song against this mutiny of trees.*
There was one that hypnotized us all—a tree
in a garden deep in the navel of Calcutta.
A banyan whose canopy holds the hair of Calcutta,
whose heart rotted in 1925, but imagine—the tree
still lives on. And this is the dream,
isn't it? To survive the anarchy of dreams?

For nights after my return, I dream
of vacant jute mills and that warrior tree.
And I hear you in each of my dreams,
pounding the hallways—do houses dream?
I'd offer every street in every city I've been, brother,
to know what forests live in your dreams,
because when you storm through my dreams,
it is a haiku of light, staining through the decay
of every long, inglorious night. O decay,
O city of supposed joy—be still and let me dream.
I bolt the doors when I return from Calcutta,
but you're walking through them all, Calcutta—

hoping to ensnare the boy. Calcutta,
you think you're going to pour your song of decay
into his delicate ears, but my brother—
he can't be seduced by your trees or your poetry.
So stampede on, great city. Dream another dream.

Understanding My Fate in a Mexican Museum

I met my past and future selves in a museum in Mexico.
In Mexico I was told it was possible to move in time
and space simultaneously, so I wasn't alarmed to see
that long-ago brooding, skinny self, or the Future Me
taking mescaline, holding a coat of flayed skin.
I'd hoped for greater scale, but still. Listen—

we wandered around, the three of us, listening
to the history of Olmec heads, and how in Mexico,
the lines between the living and the dead are thin as skin.
My past self, partial to the practices of earlier times,
marvelled at distended thighs and necklaces. For me,
she said, it all points to the glories of motherhood. See

here—interjected Future Me. All these breasts you see,
and phalluses. All this fertility flagellation, for what? Listen,
Sister, sex may be important, but babies aren't for me.
It's tough to undermine the insistences of time in Mexico.
In Mexico you can repeat yourself a million times
and still be singing through your bones and skin

like the goddess Cihuateotl, she of serpent skin—
patron saint of those who die while giving birth. We see
her in a cage of glass, palms upturned, singing of a time
when mother spirits spun like warriors with the sun. Listen
to this excellent promotion of motherhood. In Mexico
they used to worship skirts—reminding me

of my own country's zeal for female deities. Me?
I think it's all been subjugated, fumigated, skinned
and mutilated like those girls in the barrios. In Mexico
they have a name for it: *Feminicidio.* I long to see
a clearer vision for wayward women who list
between the knowing and unknowing. In time,

dear past and future selves—in time
we will resolve our joint concerns. Just leave me
for a moment with these Aztec gods to listen
at the crossroads. I may never hold creation in my skin
but I will always dream it. This is the fate I see
for my selves and me in a Mexican museum. In Mexico

I offered up my coat of skin for a chance to see
the Future Me. And in that raw, bedraggled light of Mexico
I saw a woman vanquishing the bones of time. And I listened.

Dinner Conversations

We never talked about whether Jains
were okay with electric crematoriums
when I was younger. These days even
the chairs have opinions on mortality,
speak with certainty, like people
who are convinced they know exactly
which mosquito gave them dengue.
I'm not sure what to make of the world
when someone opens the fridge for a carton
of milk, greets his wife and daughters,
Morning Girls! then drops to the floor.
I don't know if falling asleep in Banaras
and never waking up is better than slamming
your head on a San Francisco pavement
by mistake. And how to respond to Father,
who starts up about the little time he has left
when I finally announce I'm getting hitched.
The years grow drowsy on antibiotics
and you'd think we'd be counting our beloveds
just to make sure they've still got teeth in their skulls.
Never mind the floods, never mind the sludge-
torn vessels. You'd think we'd be giving up on sugar
and taking our lungs for a walk. I'm scared
I'll die in a stupid way, by choking on a cornflake,
when what I want is to be prefixed by majesty—

Her Majesty or her majestic hips could kill…
but what I get might be a raft floating out to sea,
nothing that is over indefinitely,
because here is Brother, earlobes wet
from a shower, hands full of friends—
a gentleman's navy sock, a kerchief of silk,
robberies of restaurant serviettes.
He holds them at the table's edge,
swishing them this way and that
till all our fears are a kind of hunger—
belly of wolf, eyes of wolf kings,
always asking for more more more

The Leather of Love

after John Berger

This morning I take the weathered
secateurs to stems of lantana as
a woman sometimes must. At the gate
a bee-eater suns himself and posts
a kiss to the breeze sidling on by.
Me in batik house-wrap from a departures
lounge. Bird in feathers. The strange and
marbled green of our kingdom. *Embrace the
day, bird,* I whisper. Just then white
clouds pass by, devastated as ghosts.
Bird and I look upwards. The sky's the size of
a wrinkle—winnowing and closing, the
way an absence will. Birdie's gone—
disappeared—who knows where, wrapped
in the morning's foreboding. Dragonflies in
drag, a water pump muffled by tarpaulins,
the sand and salt and shrub—this is what we
live with. And when we lie in bed and talk
of the body's failings, of the petulant dead, of
disenchantment and insufficient passion,
we're chewing through fears so thick our
teeth are beginning to rust. Passion's
how a poem's meant to breathe—the
air sacs funnelling life into saline

lungs. *Come back!* I won't be like that woman in
the rhyme who swallows a bird, which
isn't to say you aren't delectable. You, who hides
in the foliage. Yoo hoo! You, who are
the czar of colour. The morning's hung
itself on a granite obelisk, waiting for you to
reappear. I pour light through my hands to make
brass, a bell, something to lure you from
your hiding place. I, who thought a
poem could be about a garden, a staple or hinge
on which another poem could be built. I, of
limited imagination. I offer you my skin,
which is the same as offering you the
universe that breathes wild, through leather,
that sews our stomachs to gunny bags of
love. Always and only is a poem about love.

O Great Beauties!

O fatty dishes of love! — Wisława Szymborska

O Great Beauties, I have encountered
you in museums across the world,
observed you and your ilk burst against frames—
bonneted, corseted, hiding from rain.

I've coveted your wardrobes of lace
and silk. Dreamt of renaissance gowns
and acres of pickadils. O the majesty of ruff,
of petticoat tails, mantuas, farthingales!

Not to mention the excellent headgear!
Fontages and feathers, chignons and wigs.
And the sleeves, such a dizzying variety of sleeves!
Slashed, dropped, poofy, fastened back.

In my study of beauty I've also made note
of the suitable props of babies and embroidery,
viola da gambas, pianofortes, hankies,
to distract or accentuate bosoms, according

to the chronology of fashion. Of the paleness
of brow, and eyes riven with requisite
sadness as Pooch snores gaily at your feet.
But Ladies, fripperies aside, I must hasten.

I must ask dear daughters of important houses,
heroines of epics, Helens, whores, how did you know
to obscure your true selves? Wherefrom the maturity
to swallow your grins and hide your teeth?

Even you—Ms Cornelia Burch, barely two
months old, oppressed in swaddling bands
clutching your shark-toothed golden rinkelbel.
How did you perfect the art of staring so well?

Were there sisters banned from immortality
for being too tan or toothy? For guffawing
into their hands while the maestro said, *Please,
Madame, a little concentration on the stand!*

O golden-haired girls scoured of make-up,
could you know that your direct descendants
would dismiss your resplendence; call you
plain Jane, or worse: Munter, Minger?

That the gargantuan fortress of your lives
could be captured so clearly in a single portrait?
I mean no disregard, Beauties, to the centuries
of devotion to serious women.

Just explain the mystery to me.
Did darkness burn all around?
Or did you see, as I see—a quiet wood
outside the town, with a banquet

in a field of belladonna? Did spirits slide
among trees with amulets and potions,
loosening the knots of emotion in your throat,
stomach, tongue, lip, larynx, palate, jaw?

Did you strip the mutinies of silk
from the ridges of your ungodly body,
revel in tufts of skin and hair while the hunt
blazed around the edges of the lair?

And when the night-hag finally arrived,
did you invite her to bed, offer her a carafe
of your finest red, open the pearls
of your mouth to the world, and laugh?

Clumps of Happiness

Whenever I find myself in a room
with cigarette burns in the coverlets
and windows as large and heartless
as Goya's black paintings—windows
that look onto pea-shaped swimming
pools around which boisterous families
gather with cries of mummy-daddy,
which later manifest into karaoke &
Bollywood tunes, I allow myself a moment
of despair before swaddling my being
in stinky sheets and thanking he whom
I don't believe in for being a poet.
For not being in the nicer hotel
with the best-sellers and Booker-prize
winners who bite into club sandwiches
from room service and run amuck
with the minibar, whose showers
don't spray directly onto the commode.
Because if it weren't for this mouse-spiced
air, this particular desire to be anywhere
but here, how else to turn the howl
into song? How else to trawl through
tundra and beach, excavating vast,
treeless stretches for clumps of happiness?

Meeting Elizabeth Bishop in Madras

So far from Worcester, Massachusetts.
Elizabeth—you, here! At my dentist's
in Madras, sitting with pressed knees,
leafing through back copies of *Femina*.
Teeth haven't changed much, except
now we have comfort sedation for root
canals, so there's little reason to cry,
which doesn't occlude the possibility
for epiphany, just makes it harder for
empathy to pass between you and I.

The waiting room is cool and bright,
full of brown sofas, bad art, bony
teenagers with braces. You really shouldn't
be reading those magazines full of women
with their horrifying breasts, plumped up
with silicone, poised like bouncy castles
on their chests. What can possibly be gleaned
from Bebo's diet and make-up tricks? Or Kat's
wardrobe must-haves. What kind of fucked-up
message is: You can be your own Barbie?

Has it always been like this? Women
succumbing to other women, wanting
to inhabit other voices, other tongues.
Must we dream our dreams and have them too?
And you Elizabeth—you might have fallen
in February 1918, through the pages of a *National
Geographic*, through Florida and Brazil, through
geographies of heaven and hell. Through Lota
and loneliness and a million stinging arguments.
Yet here you are. Isn't this togetherness?

I speak to myself all the time, like a crazed
woman on the streets. Sometimes I sob
at train stations and wonder—will someone
console me? But eyes mostly glaze and flicker
like hummingbirds, quickly away.
And what can be said about darkness after all?
About men who board buses with iron rods?
What can be said about all the dragging and laying
of bodies to earth? Of landfills of lacerated breasts
and vaginal scree, of girls hanging from a mango tree?

What unity can there be between them
and you and me? What's real isn't what connects
our meagre horizons, but how we're moving
constantly, a colony of lemmings. At the dentist's
today, I took the bit between my teeth, and what
the X-ray showed was a picture of the future.
Stalactites growing from the soil of my gums—
tenuous, skeletal, telling me that one day I'll die;
that the dust of everyone I've ever known
will lie in graveyards or cremation grounds.

It wouldn't matter then—all the flossing
and scraping of tongues, all our universal cries
of suffering. None of it will make the dead sing
sweeter. But living, we must rush to see the sun
the other way around, we must feast on miracles
for breakfast. And even though the million
wild ascending shadows will not be back,
Elizabeth, we must engrave the words on cages,
swim through the beast of this salty knowledge.
Our art is worth this much at least.

Grandmothers Abroad

You will see them pacing platform tracks,
at corner stores, and in the park,
pushing kids about in prams,
always first to get on board.
You will see them walk the dog,
pretending to be nonchalant
about the plastic bags
they've got tied around their hands.
You will see them at markets
in pursuit of perfect fruits,
taking breaks on city benches
in saris and salwar suits.
You will see them luxuriate
in cricket scores and royal scandals,
at the bus-stop with the shopping,
edging home in socks and sandals.

You will see them, then you won't.
The plumage of their sari tails
devoured by hues of black and grey,
the outwardness of Kanchivaram
not quite right for mid-sized Durham.
You will see them scourged of colour,
bandaged in their daughter's fleeces,
hounded by their sons and nieces

to put away the jewellery pieces.
You will want to tell them to resist,
at least, the flaccid slacks and pumps that wait,
the visits to the Oxfam shops.
Granny, don't become that omnipresent
migrant woman, stripped of all her memories.
Find a courtyard filled with sun
and let your gold relentlessly
unfold upon the paisley sleeves
of your bereaved imaginings.

Poem for a Dead Dog

I want to lift you from the sand
the way a harmattan ploughs
the hell out of a Nigerian street.
To know you the way lovers
in the first blush of heat will speak
of the animals they want to be
in the next life—elephant, hippo,
always grand in design. But life,
even though it's ours, is mostly
small. Small the way I squash ants
against a wall. I want to tie a rope
around your neck and lead you
somewhere, but the way you're lying
so close to the waves, your limbs
in some complicated Pilates position...
Understand, I can't have my dogs
see you this way, it would ruin
their self-confidence. Don't think
it's because I don't believe
in hard work. I jog most mornings,
and when I read, I beat my chin
if it sags into submission.
This isn't about resisting,
but about longing, how it enters
the body, shimmying between ribs.

The body, always the body—
of you, of my dogs hovering around you,
sniffing, squatting, pissing,
tearing away to play Cowboys and
Indians because a herd of young
bulls has just appeared over the dunes,
their buff brown bodies glorious
as applause on the horizon.
Even the stranger's perfect body
you must have imagined
giving yourself over and over
to in the dark, the way all of it
creates a knob of desire.
The body left out in a week of rain,
still parched, still longing for someone
to crawl in and close the shutters.
The body offering itself to the sea.
Impossible to think there will be
no more cool mornings or summer
nights of wild moonlight loving.
Listen, someone is pounding the door.
Tell them to bring the roses in.

Find the Poets

I arrived in a foreign land yesterday,
a land that has seen troubles,
        (who hasn't, you might say?).
This land
with its scrubbed white houses
and blue seas, where everything was born,
and now, everything seems as if it could vanish—
I wanted to find out the truth
about how a great land like this
could allow ancient columns to crumble
and organ grinders to disappear.

Find the poets, my friend said.
If you want to know the truth, find the poets.

But friend, where do I find the poets?
In the soccer fields,
        at the sea shore,
                in the bars, drinking?

Where do the poets live these days,
        and what do they sing about?

I looked for them in the streets of Athens,
at the flea market and by the train station,
I thought one of them might have sold me a pair of sandals.

But he did not speak to me of poetry,

only of his struggles, of how his house was taken
from him, of all the dangers his children must now
be brave enough to face.

Find the poets, my friend said.

They will not speak of the things you and I speak about.
They will not speak of economic integration
or fiscal consolidation.

They could not tell you anything
about the burden of adjustment.

But they could sit you down
and tell you how poems are born in silence
and sometimes, in moments of great noise;
of how they arrive like the rain,
unexpectedly cracking open the sky.

They will talk of love, of course,
as if it were the only thing that mattered,
about chestnut trees and mountain tops,
and how much they miss their dead fathers.

They will talk as they have been talking
for centuries, about holding the throat of life,
till all the sunsets and lies are choked out,
till only the bones of truth remain.

The poets, my friend, are where they have always been—
living in paper houses along rivers
and in forests that are disappearing.

And while you and I go on with life
remembering and forgetting,

the poets remain: singing, singing.

The Day Night Died

bats, voles and vampires threatened
to strike. Insomnia leaned over a balcony,
shrieking, *What the...?* before vanishing
into a wormhole created by Jan Van Eyck.
Stars exposed themselves like pervs.
Forests under duress released
nyctohylophobia from their nerves.
Bonfires staged a minor revolt.
Sea said, *I'm done,* and rolled herself
back to a valley of plums. Discos
and motels schemed to Take Back
the Night, but got knifed by Brutus
in broad you-know light. Houses
reared up and slammed their blinds shut.
Dreams free-associated in corridors
of smut. Dadaists shrank against mighty
Surrealists. Jung went for Freud in the sands
of a kabaddi pit. And it was only until
the Subconscious stepped in, with
what looked like the world's tiniest violin,

whose strings she plucked like Lolita
grown up, that everyone fled from the room
in their heads, to a field where an almost extinct
species called poets, previously known
for worshipping the moon,
sat in a churlish circle of gloom.
Dead is dead, is what they said.

Coastal Life

It takes years of coastal living to understand
that you are the lifeless Malacca snake
discarded from the fisherman's net,
buried in sand. That you are connected
to the million ephemera wings, clogging
the balcony drains. That seasons will bring
rotting carapace of turtle, decapitated
tree frogs, acres of slain mosquitoes.
All night the electricity surges and stops,
smothering wires and fuses, while lizards
plop. The resident mouse leaves imprints
of his teeth on banana skins, knowing
that soon, quite soon, he will succumb
to the poisoned biscuits we lay out for him.
Underground—roots of bougainvillea
delicately throttle the water pipes,
and as if sensing this menace, the dogs,
uneasy in sleep, move their frantic legs
against concrete in pursuit of a chicken.
Even the doorjambs, plump with rain,
know that something is coming to prise
open our caskets, unhinge us with salt.
We can latch all the windows and doors
but the sea still hears us, moves towards
our bodies, our beds—hoarsely,

under guidance of the moon, with green
and white frothy arms to garland us,
with pins to mount the beasts of our lives
against a filigreed blanket of rust.

The View from Inside My Coffin

You think it's death
I'm talking about? — Dean Young

I think about whether this is real
or whether it's a kind of therapy.
Maybe I'm Korean with memory loss.
Maybe I didn't appreciate life enough,
so I dressed in white and wrote letters
to my wife before climbing in here
with a picture of myself. Maybe those videos
they made us watch of cancer survivors
and limbless people flailing around
in swimming pools will shame me
into smelling the daffodils.
But I look at the picture I'm hugging,
and I'm not Korean, I'm me.
And there's Joseph Brodsky
in the corner, talking to the ghost
of his coccyx. *Cuckoo, cuckoo,*
he's saying to the imaginary vestige.
He thinks the reason we have memory
is because we lost our tails in the race
for progress. *Cuckoo, we move because*
of you. And hearing these evocations

my fidgety toes decide to adjudicate
on migration because the weather here
is awful—pelting heat, with an always high
chance of afternoon rain. Left foot votes Canada,
right, Australia. Husband is here too,
weighing in on the world. *If you look at the lapels*
of a jacket, you'll see, it's really a representation
of labia. Men in their power suits all being born.
Think of the millions of labia. He's Italian so...
And on a Karmic observational note:
it's crowded in here for someone who suffers
from claustrophobia.
                                    The thing they say
about your hair and nails? That's true.
But who knew even frown lines continue
to grow? There's a ditch in the middle
of my head that's beginning to worry me.
And no one so far has been able to explain
cruelty to me. Not the maggots or the Ramanujans—
there's two of them here—the poet
and the genius, both lurching towards infinity
through flimsy routes of nothingness.
O zero, O body, O yes, I know enough
about the universe to know I carry it
within me, but what I really need
is to get out of this yoga vortex.
Tell me: was it necessary to bite that girl
in school when all she was being

is friendly? And why in life's tough
moments did I need to just lie down?
What does that say about decency?
          The mood here is very James Turrell.
Very underground museum where they make you
walk corridors with bags on your feet.
So, of course, hush, of course, wonder.
And when they guide you up the steps
to gaze into a field of mirrors,
there can be no doubt that what you're looking at
is life, and when you turn back into the dark,
it's either the future or the past,
but most probably it's death.
                    Since you ask,
what I miss about the everyday
is the strain of getting by, the drag and pull
of gears like a car in second when it should
be in fourth. And the only shame I'll confess
to is staring too hard at the washing machine
as it spin cycles into orgasm.
For the rest, let the record state
that my desire to embody a Russian icon painting
has finally come true. Here, on the inside,
I see that perspective is skewed,
and there's a box for everything.

Portrait of the Poet as a Reclining God

Don't make much of the fact that recline
rhymes with decline. Do it anyway.
Stretch out sideways. Think Titian's
Venus, but with clothes. Better still,
think Hindu gods. Press mound
of palm up to lake of ear. Imagine
legs of blue, legs of Vishnu,
serpent skin susurrating against
your back. Belly? But of course,
Ganesha's. Breasts or no breasts,
that is the question. Ardhanarishvara.
Grow serious as we sweep towards
the eyes. Focus inwards, Avalokiteshvara.
Cradle that palm against your ear as if
it were a telephone. Whisper into the velvet
air: *Hello heart! You still there?*

When I Was Still a Poet

When I was still a poet
I used to dream of rivers.
Flowers had names and
purpose. Small birds
the shape of scars
made nests in braziers
of sky. Now that I
have given up,
afternoons dry
as raisin skins scrub
by. Thieves approach.
Dogs bark. Love springs
from dirt like carrots.

ACKNOWLEDGEMENTS

Grateful acknowledgment is made to the editors of the following publications: *Abbreviate, Asia Literary Review, Departures, February Anthology, Filigree: A New Anthology of Contemporary Black British Poetry, Fulcrum, Granta, Golden Shovel Anthology, The Guardian, The Indian Quarterly, Kavya Bharati, Kindle, LA.LIT, Liberty, Magma, Poetry, Poetry at Sangam, Poetry Wales, The Long White Thread of Words: Poems for John Berger.*

'How to be Happy in 101 Days' was commissioned by the United Nations Society of Writers to commemorate the International Day of Happiness, and appeared in the anthology, *Happiness, The Delight-Tree.*

Thanks to Terrance Hayes for inventing the Golden Shovel form, used in 'Strong Men, Riding Horses' and 'The Leather of Love'.

Both aphorisms used in 'Your Body Language is Not Indian!' are by Nicolás Gómez Dávila.

'The View from Inside My Coffin' was inspired by a news story about how South Koreans are combatting suicide rates with coffin therapy.

The book's epigraph taken from 'January' is reproduced with permission from Bloodaxe Books, *R.S. Thomas, Selected Poems 1948-1968* (Bloodaxe Books, 1986).

ABOUT THE AUTHOR

Tishani Doshi publishes novels, essays and poetry. She has worked as a dancer with the Chandralekha troupe for fifteen years. She lives on a beach in Tamil Nadu.

www.tishanidoshi.com

Poetry is vital to language and living. Since 1972, Copper Canyon Press has published extraordinary poetry from around the world to engage the imaginations and intellects of readers, writers, booksellers, librarians, teachers, students, and donors.

WE ARE GRATEFUL FOR THE MAJOR SUPPORT PROVIDED BY:

THE PAUL G. ALLEN
FAMILY FOUNDATION

The Chinese character for poetry is made up of two parts: "word" and "temple." It also serves as pressmark for Copper Canyon Press.

The poems are set in Adobe Caslon Pro.

CPSIA information can be obtained
at www.ICGtesting.com
Printed in the USA
LVOW11*0905030518
575745LV00002B/6/P